STECK-VAUGHN

EXERCISES

D0523068

Betty Jones
Saranna Moeller
Cynthia T. Strauch

A Subsidiary of National Education Corporation

About the Authors

Saranna S. Moeller has been a teacher in the elementary grades for over twenty-five years. Moeller received her bachelor's degree in education from the University of Houston. She now operates the Refugio Learning Center in Texas.

Betty Jones earned her master's degree in education from Prairie View A & M University. Jones has been an elementary teacher for over twenty-five years.

Cynthia T. Strauch attained her master's degree in education at Texas A & I University. Strauch is also an experienced elementary school teacher, with over sixteen years of service.

Acknowledgments

Senior Editor: Diane Sharpe

Project Editor: Stephanie Muller

Product Development: The Wheetley Company, Inc.

Cover Design: Sue Heatly Design

Illustrations: Michael Krone

Photography: p. 3 Bill Records; p. 4 Sandy Wilson; p. 15 Michael Patrick; p. 20 Florida News Bureau; p. 25 Space Photos; p. 27 Miami Beach News Bureau; p. 34 Craig Jobson; p. 39 Loren McIntyre

LANGUAGE EXERCISES Series:

Level A/Pink	Level D/Gray	Level G/Gold
Level B/Orange	Level E/Red	Level H/Green
Level C/Violet	Level F/Blue	Review/Yellow

ISBN 0-8114-4192-X

Copyright © 1990 National Education Corporation.
All rights reserved. No part of the material protected by this copyright may be reproduced or utilized in any form or by any means, electronic or mechanical, including photocopying, recording, or by any information storage and retrieval system, without permission in writing from the copyright owner. Requests for permission to make copies of any part of the work should be mailed to: Copyright Permissions, Steck-Vaughn Company, P.O. Box 26015, Austin, TX 78755. Printed in the United States of America.

4 5 6 7 8 9 0 HG 95 94 93 92

Table of Contents

UNIT 1 Vocabulary

UNIT 2 Sentences

UNIT 3 Grammar and Usage

UNIT 4 Capitalization and Punctuation

UNIT 5 Composition

UNIT 6 Study Skills

Final Reviews

Synonyms 1

- A **synonym** is a word that means almost the same thing as another word.
  EXAMPLE: small—little

- **Write a synonym for each underlined word. Choose the synonyms from the box.**

1. Don't push and ________________ people in line.
2. Throw the dime to me, or ________________ it to Roberto.
3. The lid is closed and ________________ tight.
4. Touch the cup, and ________________ how hot it is.
5. She got a large banana, but couldn't finish it because it was so ________________.
6. The apple is bright and ________________.
7. The lunchroom is loud and ________________.
8. Did you choose a spoon or ________________ a fork?
9. That silly joke is ________________.
10. Eric fell in a muddy puddle and got his clothes ________________.

dirty
feel
funny
huge
noisy
pick
shiny
shove
shut
toss

- **Write a sentence using the synonyms great and wonderful. Tell about something you like.**

____

____

Antonyms 2

- An **antonym** is a word that means the opposite of another word.
  EXAMPLE: on—off

- **Circle the antonym for each underlined word.**

1. The show is before spring break but (after, during) the art fair.
2. Will it be dark or (heavy, light) outside when the show is over?
3. Myron said that flips were easy but handstands were (safe, hard).
4. The baby was asleep during the first part of the program, but (awake, sleepy) during the second.
5. Some of the music will be slow, and other music will be (quiet, fast).

- **Write the sentences. Complete each one with an antonym for the underlined word.**

1. Do you think Ann will win or (lose, leave)?

   ____

   ____

2. Will he do a backbend now or (never, later)?

   ____

   ____

Homonyms 3

- A **homonym** is a word that sounds the same as another word but has a different spelling and a different meaning.

  EXAMPLES: **they're, their, there**

  Use they're to mean "they are."

  They're playing now.

  Use their to mean "belonging to them."

  Did they bring **their** bats?

  Use there to mean "in that place" or to help begin a thought.

  He threw it **there. There** are two teams.

- **Write they're, their, or there.**

1. Lee and Vin raced down the street carrying ____________________ baseball gloves.

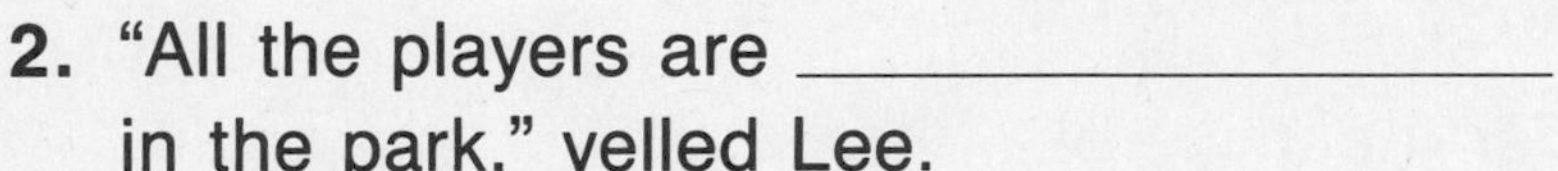

2. "All the players are ____________________ in the park," yelled Lee.
3. "I hope ____________________ ready for the big game today," said Vin.
4. All the players quickly took ____________________ places on the field.
5. "Look, ____________________ are people cheering for us!" cried Vin.
6. "I think ____________________ here to see us win the game," said Lee.
7. Vin and Lee's team won ____________________ game by one point.

- **Write a sentence about a ball game using they're, their, or there.**

____

More Homonyms 4

- Remember that a homonym is a word that sounds the same as another word.

  EXAMPLES: **hear, here** **to, two, too**

  Use hear to mean "to listen to."
  Did you **hear** that funny song?
  Use here to mean "in this place."
  The tapes are over **here.**

  Use to to mean "toward" or to go with words like make and buy.
  Juan rode his bike **to** the store. He wanted **to** buy a tape.
  Use too to mean "more than enough" or "also."
  The music is **too** loud. I like that song, **too.**
  Use two to mean "the number 2."
  Those **two** speakers sound very good.

- **Underline the correct homonym.**

  1. Put the new speakers over (hear, here).
  2. Listen (to, too, two) the soft music.
  3. Do you (hear, here) the band play?
  4. Those (to, too, two) records were on sale.
  5. Dad bought some tapes, (to, too, two).
  6. We will dance when we (hear, here) the music.
  7. Mom will come in (to, too, two) watch us.
  8. (Here, Hear) comes Dad to show us a dance.
  9. His (to, too, two) feet just float across the floor.
  10. Do you (hear, here) us clapping for him?

- **Use hear and here in a sentence about music.**

____

Words with More Than One Meaning 5

- Many words have more than one meaning.
  EXAMPLE: Pound means "a weight equal to 16 ounces." Buy a **pound** of peanuts. Pound also means "hit hard over and over." **Pound** the stake into the ground.

- **Read the meanings on the right. Write the number of the meaning for each underlined word.**

1. My little brother was playing with his spinning top. _____
2. Mom asked him to turn on the outside light. _____
3. The strong wind had turned over the light doghouse. _____
4. I heard the dog bark at the squirrel. _____
5. It was climbing up the bark of the tree. _____
6. The squirrel went to the top of the tree. _____
7. The branch was almost too light to hold the squirrel. _____
8. But there wasn't enough light to see where the squirrel went next. _____

light
1. not heavy
2. something by which we see

bark
1. hard outside covering of a tree
2. the sound a dog makes

top
1. the highest part
2. a toy

- **Write a sentence using the first meaning of light.**

____

____

Prefixes **6**

- A **prefix** is a word part added to the beginning of a base word to change the meaning of the word.

  EXAMPLES: The prefix un- means "not" or "the opposite of." The prefix re- means "again."

  un- + usual = **un**usual, meaning "not usual"

  re- + heat = **re**heat, meaning "heat again"

- **Add the prefix un- to the words below.**
  Then write the meaning of the new word.

1. happy ______________ ______________________

2. fair ______________ ______________________

3. even ______________ ______________________

4. safe ______________ ______________________

5. tie ______________ ______________________

- **Add the prefix re- to the words below.**
  Then write the meaning of the new word.

1. open ______________ ______________________

2. test ______________ ______________________

3. use ______________ ______________________

4. read ______________ ______________________

- **Write one sentence with a word that has the prefix un-.**
  Write one sentence with a word that has the prefix re-.

1. ____

2. ____

Suffixes 7

- A **suffix** is a word part added to the end of a base word to change the meaning of the word.

  EXAMPLES: The suffixes -er and -or mean "a person or thing that ___."

  heat + -er = heat**er**, meaning "a thing that heats"

  sail + -or = sail**or**, meaning "a person that sails"

- **Add the suffixes to the words to make new words.**

1. climb + er = ________________
2. teach + er = ________________
3. visit + or = ________________
4. travel + er = ________________
5. act + or = ________________
6. mark + er = ________________
7. paint + er = ________________
8. sing + er = ________________

- **Write each sentence with a new word made by adding -er to the word in ( ).**

1. The ___ clipped the roses. (garden)

   ____

2. He cleaned his gloves in the ___. (wash)

   ____

3. He and a ___ ate lunch. (farm)

   ____

4. Then he hired a new ___ to help him. (work)

   ____

5. The new worker used to be a ___. (teach)

   ____

Compound Words 8

- A **compound word** is made by joining one word with another word.
  EXAMPLE: air + plane = airplane

- **Write the compound word made by joining each pair of words.**

1. birth + day = ______________________
2. after + noon = ______________________
3. skate + board = ______________________
4. fire + place = ______________________
5. cat + fish = ______________________
6. rain + bow = ______________________
7. snow + ball = ______________________
8. sun + rise = ______________________
9. water + fall = ______________________
10. down + stairs = ______________________

- **Underline the compound word in each sentence. Then write the two words that form the compound word.**

1. The birthday party is a surprise. ____________ ____________
2. Is everyone here? ____________ ____________

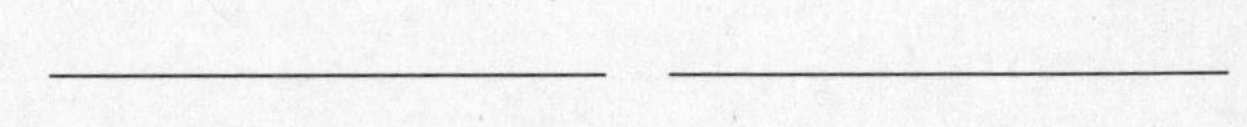

3. Let's run downstairs and hide! ____________ ____________

4. Everything is ready. ____________ ____________

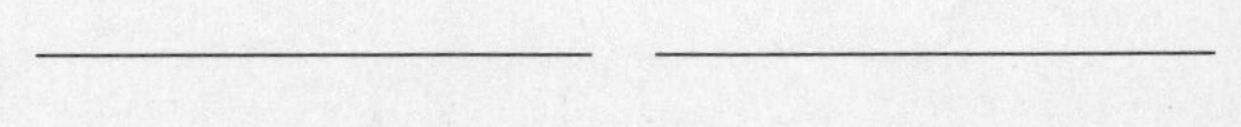

5. The party is for a classmate. ____________ ____________
6. I brought a football as a gift. ____________ ____________

Contractions 9

- A **contraction** is a word made by joining two words. When the words are joined, a letter or letters are left out. An **apostrophe** (') shows where the missing letter or letters would be.

  EXAMPLES: I + will = I'll, there + is = there's, is + not = isn't

- **Rewrite the sentences. Use contractions in place of the underlined words.**

doesn't	Here's	I'll	isn't	she'll	She's	There's

1. She is going camping this weekend.

   ____

2. I think she will go fishing in the lake.

   ____

3. Inuk does not like to fish.

   ____

4. Here is some fresh bait.

   ____

5. There is enough for everyone to use.

   ____

6. After we catch the fish, I will help cook.

   ____

7. It is not hard to do.

   ____

- **Write a sentence telling what you will do this weekend. Use the contraction I'll.**

____

Review

- **Write the synonym for each underlined word.**

1. The small dog stars in a circus. (tiny, big) ______________________

2. Sparky does some simple tricks. (hard, easy) ______________________

- **Write the antonym for each underlined word.**

1. The clown is happy, but has a (sad, red) face. ______________________

2. Was Bozo's wink fast or (quick, slow)? ______________________

- **Choose and underline the correct word in each sentence.**

1. The dancing bear is over (here, hear).

2. The stars took (they're, their, there) bows.

3. Darla has fun at the circus, (to, too, two).

- **Write two sentences. Use a different meaning for pound in each sentence.**

1. ____

2. ____

- **Underline each word that begins with a prefix.**

1. pack, unpack **2.** true, untrue **3.** relive, live

- **Underline each word that ends with a suffix.**

1. clean, cleaner **2.** visitor, visit **3.** teacher, teach

- **Underline each contraction. Circle each compound word.**

1. There's the tightrope. **2.** We'll be inside the tent.

Using What You've Learned

- **Rewrite the letter. Use a homonym for the words in dark print. Use a contraction for the words that are underlined.**

> Dear Tom,
>
> It was very hot **hear** in the house today. I went **too** the pool **too** cool off. My **to** friends, Anna and Rosa, were **their.** We did not do anything but swim. We will go back tomorrow. I **here** it will be even hotter then. I will be sure to tell Anna and Rosa to bring **they're** beach ball.

- **Write a story about summer fun. Include these words in your story:**

1. a synonym of bright
2. an antonym of cold
3. the homonyms pale, pail
4. a compound word
5. a word with the prefix re- or un-
6. a word with the suffix -er or -or

Sentences 10

- A **sentence** is a group of words that tells or asks something. It stands for a complete thought.
  EXAMPLE: Sally dreamed about the picnic.

- **Underline the sentences.**

1. Eva and Sue ate fried chicken.
2. Smelled good to eat.
3. Did Sue find the rolls?
4. Sue and Eva?
5. Eva ran to get a swing.
6. Swung up to the stars.
7. Is Sue hungry again?
8. Potato salad.

- **Match each group of words in A with a group of words in B to make a complete sentence. Write the sentences below.**

A	B
The ants	looking for crumbs.
They were	marched in a row.
Eva	saw them coming.
She moved	was for Eva, not the ants.
The food	her blanket right away.

1. ________________________
2. ________________________
3. ________________________
4. ________________________
5. ________________________

Identifying Sentences 11

- Remember that a sentence is a group of words that tells or asks something. It stands for a complete thought.

- **Choose the sentence in each pair of word groups below. Write the sentence.**

1. Catherine saw Superdog. A most unusual dog.

    ____

2. Flew high as a rocket. Superdog flew high.

    ____

3. Where is Superdog? Superdog with his cape?

    ____

4. Superdog read about the dog show. The big show.

    ____

5. Went to the show. Superdog went to the show.

    ____

6. Win a ribbon? Did he win a blue ribbon?

    ____

7. Superdog won "Best of Show." "Best of Show."

    ____

- **Read the paragraph below. Draw a line through each group of words that is not a sentence.**

Catherine and Superdog walked to the dog show. What did Superdog do there? Surprised all the judges. The judges in the chairs. Superdog ran as fast as a train. Jumped over a tall building in a single bound.

Statements and Questions 12

- Some sentences are **statements.** They tell something.
  EXAMPLE: Hawaii is a beautiful state.
- Some sentences are **questions.** They ask something.
  EXAMPLE: Is Hawaii a beautiful state?

- **Write S in front of each statement.**
  Write Q in front of each question.

_____ **1.** Hawaii has many miles of beaches.

_____ **2.** Does Hawaii have over a hundred islands?

_____ **3.** The sun shines there on most days.

_____ **4.** Many kinds of flowers grow in Hawaii.

_____ **5.** Do farmers grow pineapples?

_____ **6.** Sugarcane is an important crop in Hawaii.

_____ **7.** Hawaii is called the Aloha State.

_____ **8.** "Aloha" is a Hawaiian greeting.

_____ **9.** Would you like to go to Hawaii?

_____ **10.** When do you want to go?

- **Copy the sentences below. Underline the statement once. Underline the question twice.**

Many people visit Hawaii to ride the waves. Which beach do they like best?

____

____

____

Commands and Exclamations 13

- Some sentences are **commands.** They tell somebody to do something.
  EXAMPLE: Squeeze all the juice out of the lemons.
- Some sentences are **exclamations.** They show strong feelings or surprise.
  EXAMPLE: What a sour taste that lemon has!

- **Write C in front of each command. Write E in front of each exclamation.**

_____ **1.** How delicious those strawberries look!

_____ **2.** Slice the bananas.

_____ **3.** Add the water to the mix.

_____ **4.** What a great lunch we'll have outside!

_____ **5.** Clean the grill well.

_____ **6.** How golden that chicken is!

_____ **7.** Pass the salad, please.

_____ **8.** The ants got the cake!

_____ **9.** What a good idea this picnic was!

- **Write a sentence that is a command. Tell somebody to do the first step in making your favorite food.**

____

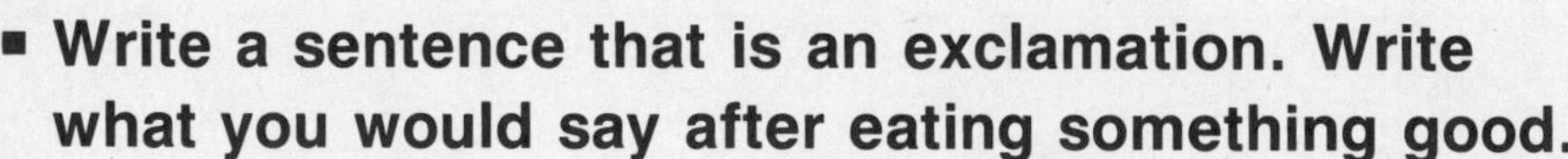

- **Write a sentence that is an exclamation. Write what you would say after eating something good.**

____

Subjects in Sentences 14

- A sentence has two parts. One part is called the **subject.** The subject tells who or what the sentence is about. EXAMPLE: **The snow** is deep.

- **Underline the subject in each sentence.**

1. We went sledding today.
2. The sled flew down the hill.
3. Val threw a snowball.
4. Stan lost his hat.
5. Skaters were on the pond.
6. The ice was smooth.
7. Percy liked to spin around.
8. He went very fast.
9. The girls slid by us.
10. A red glove was in the snow.

- **Complete each sentence by adding a subject.**

1. ______________________ put on her ice skates.
2. ______________________ helped his little sister.
3. ______________________ sat on the sled.
4. ______________________ went down the hill.
5. ______________________ was very cold.
6. ______________________ watched the snow fall.
7. ______________________ liked the snow.
8. ______________________ makes tracks in the snow.
9. ______________________ are on the ice.
10. ______________________ can skate well.
11. ______________________ turned to the left.
12. ______________________ went home.

Predicates in Sentences 15

- A sentence has two parts. One part is called the subject. The other part is called the **predicate.** The predicate tells what the subject is, was, or does.
  EXAMPLE: That big zoo **is nearby.**

- **Underline the predicate in each sentence.**

1. The cub growled at the bird.
2. The huge ape swung from a bar.
3. Barry liked the camels.
4. These tiny snakes are harmless.
5. Monkeys are fun to watch.
6. Vic petted the sheep.
7. A calf was in the yard.
8. Lee saw the baby ducks.
9. The pigs cooled off.
10. An owl hooted softly.

- **Complete each sentence by adding a predicate.**

1. The clucking chickens ______________________________.
2. The baby goats ______________________________.
3. Barbara ______________________________.
4. All the elephants ______________________________.
5. A zookeeper ______________________________.
6. The bears ______________________________.
7. Those tigers ______________________________.
8. Many people ______________________________.
9. A sleeping bat ______________________________.
10. The balloon man ______________________________.
11. Everyone ______________________________.

Combining Subjects and Predicates 16

- Two short sentences with the same predicate can be **combined** to make a new sentence. The two parts are joined by and. EXAMPLE: Lou laughed. + Gina laughed. → Lou **and** Gina laughed.
- Two short sentences with the same subject can be combined to make a new sentence. The two parts are joined by and. EXAMPLE: Fred counted his coins. + Fred paid for the tickets. → Fred counted his coins **and** paid for the tickets.

- **Combine the sentences. Write the new sentence.**

1. Mom went on the ride. Tisha went on the ride.

   ____

2. Bob stood in line. The boys stood in line.

   ____

3. Lee ate lunch. Percy ate lunch.

   ____

4. Donna took a picture. Donna sat down to rest.

   ____

5. Ed popped the balloons. Ed won a prize.

   ____

6. Linda went to the petting zoo. Linda fed the animals.

   ____

   ____

7. Ryan saw the bears. Ryan rode on the train.

   ____

Combining Sentences 17

- Two short sentences that closely share an idea can be combined to make one sentence.
- The two sentences may be joined with connecting words such as <u>or</u>, <u>and</u>, or <u>but</u>. A comma is placed before these words.

  EXAMPLES: Len found shells. + Amy caught seaweed. →
  Len found shells, **and** Amy caught seaweed.
  I can't swim. + I can wade. →
  I can't swim, **but** I can wade.
  Fish from here. + Go to the dock. →
  Fish from here, **or** go to the dock.

- **Underline the two short sentences that were combined to make each sentence.**

1. The wind howled, and the sand blew around.

2. The girls can swim, or they can play ball.

3. The water is cold, but the sand is warm.

4. The sea is blue, and the foam is white.

5. Dad carried our lunch, and we carried the chairs.

- **Combine the sentences using the word in ( ). Write the new sentence.**

1. Take your pail. Fill it with sand. (and)

____

2. You can make a castle. You can make a cave. (or)

____

3. We can't play on rocks. We can play on sand. (but)

____

Writing Clear Sentences 18

- If a sentence tells about more than one main idea, it should be rewritten as two sentences.

  EXAMPLE: Most plants have seeds, some seeds are good to eat. → Most plants have seeds. Some seeds are good to eat.

- **Read the sentences. Write two sentences for each.**

1. The plant's seeds must be thrown around, this is done in many ways.

2. A seed floated in the breeze, it was very windy.

3. You can eat these seeds, Flo will gather some more.

4. Birds and animals eat seeds, you can buy seeds for them in a store.

Review

■ **Underline the group of words that is a sentence.**

1. Owls have big eyes.
2. Catch food at night.

■ **Write S in front of the statement. Write Q in front of the question.**

_____ 1. Why did the kitten buy a fan?

_____ 2. It wanted to be a cool cat.

■ **Write C in front of the command. Write E in front of the exclamation.**

_____ 1. Give the cat its food.

_____ 2. What beautiful fur your cat has!

■ **Underline the subject. Circle the predicate.**

1. The cat washed its face with its paw.
2. Kirk threw a ball of yarn to the cat.
3. Cats take long naps.

■ **Combine the sentences to make a new sentence.**

1. Erin fed her mouse. Erin cleaned its cage.

____

____

2. Raul held the mouse. Ann held the mouse.

____

____

3. The water is cold. The sand is warm.

____

____

Using What You've Learned

- **Rewrite the story below, but make it less choppy. Combine each pair of sentences that is underlined. When you are finished, you will have six sentences in all.**

Once a tiny king lived near a huge forest. He loved to spend his days outdoors. The king chased butterflies. The king watched birds. The lords said he was a peaceful king. The ladies said he was a peaceful king. One day, the king saw a rainbow-colored bird. The bird granted him a wish. The king wished to live peacefully ever after.

- **Write a story about a king or queen who is granted a wish. Use at least two statements, one question, and one exclamation.**

- **Write a story about a wish you could be granted. Use at least two statements, one question, and one exclamation.**

Nouns 19

- A **noun** is a word that names a person, place, or thing. The words a, an, and the are clues that show a noun is near.
  EXAMPLES: a pilot, the moon, the island

- **Underline the two nouns in each sentence.**

1. The spaceman looked out the window.
2. Clouds circled the earth.
3. The ocean looked like a lake.
4. Another spaceman ate his lunch.
5. An apple floated inside the cabin.
6. One man put on his spacesuit.
7. The spaceman walked in space.
8. The newspaper had pictures of him.

- **Write a noun from the list to complete each sentence.**

best	ocean	radio
cheer	happy	ship
day	hear	tall
doctor	over	the

1. They landed in the ____________________.
2. A ____________________ sailed over to them.
3. The ____________________ checked their health.
4. The news was on the ____________________.
5. We all yelled out a ____________________.
6. It was an exciting ____________________.

Singular and Plural Nouns 20

- A **singular noun** names one person, place, or thing.
  EXAMPLES: bee, fox, bench
- A **plural noun** names more than one person, place, or thing. Add -s to most nouns to change them to mean more than one. Add -es to nouns that end with s, sh, ch, x, or z to change them to mean more than one.
  EXAMPLES: bees, foxes, benches

- **Make the nouns plural.**

1. skate ______________________
2. car ______________________
3. parade ______________________
4. toe ______________________
5. brush ______________________
6. class ______________________
7. inch ______________________
8. box ______________________
9. dish ______________________
10. dollar ______________________
11. leash ______________________
12. watch ______________________

- **Rewrite each sentence. Choose the correct noun in ( ).**

1. The fish are in a new (tank, tanks).

   ____

2. All the (plant, plants) are fresh.

   ____

3. Use that (net, nets) to catch the fish.

   ____

4. Both those (boy, boys) visit the fish store.

   ____

Common and Proper Nouns 21

- A **proper noun** names a particular person, place, or thing. It begins with a capital letter.
  EXAMPLES: George Bush, Seattle, Park School
- A **common noun** does not name a particular person, place, or thing.
  EXAMPLES: president, city, school

- **Write C for a common noun. Write P for a proper noun.**

_____ 1. girl

_____ 2. Mexico

_____ 3. mountain

_____ 4. country

_____ 5. Alabama

_____ 6. Tolman Company

_____ 7. lake

_____ 8. Helen Keller

_____ 9. Friday

_____ 10. Mojave Desert

_____ 11. building

_____ 12. doctor

- **Read the sentences. Draw one line under the common noun. Circle the proper noun.**

1. The ocean was very rough on Tuesday.
2. The waves pounded Sand Beach.
3. The beach is in Hawaii.
4. Some boys were there from Portland.
5. Julio spied a seaplane.
6. Another boy saw a Flying Eagle.
7. The plane was flying to Canada.
8. Sarah waved to the pilot.

Action Verbs 22

- A **verb** usually shows action. It tells what a person, place, or thing is or was doing.

  EXAMPLES: The cub **sleeps** in the shade.

  A tiger **ran** across the field.

- **Underline the verb in each sentence.**

  1. A beautiful bird chattered in the forest.
  2. Elephants drank from the stream.
  3. An animal leaped in the air.
  4. Meg read this in a book about Africa.
  5. She got it from the library.

- **Choose a verb from the list to complete each sentence.**

buzz	grow	roar	search	swing

1. The lions ____________________ loudly.
2. Many plants ____________________ by the stream.
3. Monkeys ____________________ from branches.
4. The insects ____________________ above us.
5. We ____________________ for butterflies.

- **Use an action verb in a sentence about animals in Africa.**

____

____

Verbs in the Present 23

- Verbs can show that an action happens in the **present.** EXAMPLE: The game **starts** now.
- Verbs in the present used with singular subjects end in -s. EXAMPLE: Troy **likes** to pitch.
- Verbs in the present used with plural subjects have no special endings. EXAMPLE: The girls **play** kickball.

Complete each sentence with the correct verb.

1. The bell ________________ at 10:00. (ring, rings)
2. The children ________________ outside to play. (run, runs)
3. Betty ________________ to Myra. (wave, waves)
4. The students ________________ to their friends. (talk, talks)
5. The new girl ________________ at the ball. (swing, swings)
6. My teacher ________________ us laugh. (make, makes)
7. Claudia ________________ a joke. (tell, tells)
8. The boys ________________ for the game. (plan, plans)

Write sentences with verbs in the present.

1. Tell what you do during recess at school.

____

____

2. Tell what other people do during recess.

____

____

Verbs in the Past

24

- Verbs can show that an action happened in the **past.** Add the endings -d or -ed to most verbs to show that something happened in the past.

  EXAMPLE: Yesterday we **washed** our bikes.

- **Underline the verb in each sentence. Write P in front of each sentence with a verb in the past.**

_____ 1. My friends like to ride to the park.

_____ 2. The wheels turned around and around.

_____ 3. They stopped at the light.

_____ 4. I squeezed the red handlebars.

_____ 5. We pedal as far as we can.

_____ 6. They rested for a half hour.

- **Rewrite the sentences. Change each verb from the present to the past by adding -d or -ed.**

1. We enter the bike race.

____

2. We start the race together.

____

3. We walk our bikes up the hill.

____

4. The dogs chase our wheels.

____

5. I hope to win.

____

Linking Verbs 25

- A **linking verb** does not show action. It links, or joins, the subject to a word in the predicate. Verbs such as <u>am</u>, <u>is</u>, <u>are</u>, <u>was</u>, and <u>were</u> are linking verbs.
  EXAMPLES: Those insects **are** crickets.
  They **were** noisy.

- **Write <u>L</u> in front of each sentence that has a linking verb.**

_____ **1.** The crickets are loud tonight.

_____ **2.** They chirp in the grass.

_____ **3.** The dogs bark at the cars.

_____ **4.** They were quiet earlier.

_____ **5.** An owl screeches in the tree.

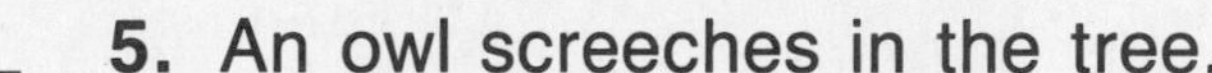

_____ **6.** It is afraid of the dogs.

_____ **7.** The white cat meows at her kitten.

_____ **8.** She tells it not to wander.

_____ **9.** The birds are asleep in their nests.

_____ **10.** A jet roars over the house.

_____ **11.** Everyone is quiet inside.

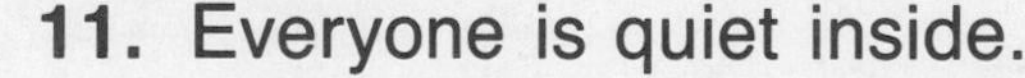

_____ **12.** Just listen to the sounds at night!

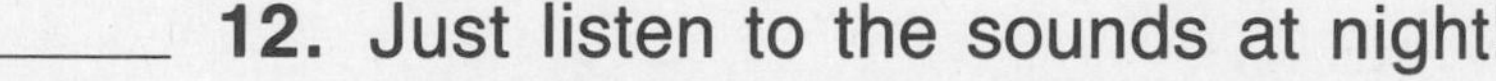

- **Use a linking verb in a sentence that tells about another sound you can hear at night.**

____

Using *Am, Is,* and *Are* 26

- Use am with the word I.
  EXAMPLE: I **am** ready to go fishing.
- Use is with one person, place, or thing.
  EXAMPLE: Joe **is** ready to go, too.
- Use are with more than one and with the word you.
  EXAMPLES: We **are** all ready now.
  Are you ready to go?

- **Write am, is, or are.**

The children __________ fishing. Joe __________ the first to catch a fish.

He says, "It __________ too small. I will put it back into the water. When I __________ a few years older, I might catch it again!"

"You __________ smart," says May. "It __________ good to throw fish back when they are too small."

"I __________ sure I have something big!" shouts Sam.

May and Joe help Sam pull the fish to the bank.

"That __________ not a fish," says May. She holds up an old tin can. "People spoil our fishing spot with junk. I __________ ready to put up a 'No Dumping' sign here."

"Two signs __________ here now," says Sam. "They __________ over there behind that pile of junk!"

Using *Was* and *Were* 27

- Use was and were to tell about the past.
- Use was with one person, place, or thing.
  EXAMPLE: Chris **was** busy in the kitchen.
- Use were with more than one and with the word you.
  EXAMPLES: The dishes **were** in the sink.
  We **were** glad that you **were** here to help.

- **Write was or were.**

1. The circus ____________ here last week.
2. Many animals ____________ there.
3. The talking birds ____________ a hit.
4. I ____________ excited to see the chicken.
5. It ____________ on roller skates.
6. A cat ____________ at the piano.
7. The frogs and toads ____________ everywhere.
8. One ____________ on an elephant.
9. The elephant ____________ in tap shoes.
10. The monkeys ____________ amazing.
11. They ____________ following the ducks and geese.
12. The ducks and geese ____________ singing.
13. A snake ____________ in a basket.
14. The horses ____________ in the center ring.
15. I ____________ very happy to be there.

Helping Verbs 28

- A **helping verb** helps the main verb. Have, has, or had helps a main verb show action in the past.

  EXAMPLES: Rita has moved to a cottage.
  They have packed their bags.
  The farmer had milked the goat.

- **Underline the helping verb. Circle the main verb.**

1. The sun has risen.
2. The roosters had remembered to crow.
3. The cows have chewed their grass.
4. The girls had collected the eggs.
5. Dad has baked some fresh bread.
6. We have eaten breakfast.

- **Rewrite the sentences using the correct verb in ( ).**

1. I (has, have) walked to the park.

   ____

2. A gentle rain (has, have) started.

   ____

3. It (has, had) rained yesterday.

   ____

4. Pat (has, had) picked out an umbrella last week.

   ____

Using Forms of *Do* and *See* 29

- Use does with a singular subject to show the present.
  EXAMPLE: Anna **does** all the costumes.
- Use do with I, you, and plural subjects to show the present.
  EXAMPLE: Al and Lyn **do** want to see the play.
- Use did without a helping verb to show the past.
  EXAMPLE: Ed **did** a play about pets.
- Use done with a helping verb to show the past.
  EXAMPLE: Fay has **done** her part.

- **Underline the correct verb.**

1. Our class (done, did) a play.
2. We had (done, did) one act.
3. Jo (does, do) well at acting.
4. Nan had (did, done) the costumes.
5. We all (does, do) a silly dance.
6. I (do, does) like to dance.

- Use sees with a singular subject to show the present.
  EXAMPLE: Anna **sees** a runner.
- Use see with I, you, and plural subjects to show the present.
  EXAMPLE: Al and Lyn **see** the first runners.
- Use saw without a helping verb to show the past.
  EXAMPLE: Ed **saw** the high jump contest.
- Use seen with a helping verb to show the past.
  EXAMPLE: Fay has **seen** a lot of track meets.

- **Underline the correct verb.**

1. We (saw, seen) a track meet today.
2. Mom said, "I (see, sees) our seats."
3. We (saw, seen) the high jump contest.
4. Di (sees, see) the last winner.
5. We all shouted, "I (see, sees) the prizes!"
6. The runners had (seen, saw) the crowd.

Using Forms of *Give* and *Go* 30

- Use gives with a singular subject to show the present.
  EXAMPLE: Anna **gives** the actors a gift.
- Use give with I, you, and plural subjects to show the present.
  EXAMPLE: Al and Lyn **give** helpful tips to the actors.
- Use gave without a helping verb to show the past.
  EXAMPLE: Ed **gave** a speech before the play.
- Use given with a helping verb to show the past.
  EXAMPLE: Fay had **given** a speech last year.

- **Underline the correct verb.**

1. They (give, gives) the play.
2. Kim (give, gives) a lot of help.
3. Our coach (gave, given) a speech.
4. He has (gave, given) it already.
5. Jim had (gave, given) a speech.
6. Our teacher (gives, give) prizes.
7. We have (gave, given) her flowers.
8. The crowd (gave, given) a cheer.

- Use goes with a singular subject to show the present.
  EXAMPLE: Anna **goes** to the zoo.
- Use go with I, you, and plural subjects to show the present.
  EXAMPLE: Al and Lyn **go** to the zoo often.
- Use went without a helping verb to show the past.
  EXAMPLE: Ed **went** to the children's zoo.
- Use gone with a helping verb to show the past.
  EXAMPLE: Fay has **gone** with Ed.

- **Underline the correct verb.**

1. We (go, goes) to the zoo.
2. Sue (go, goes) with her family.
3. I have (gone, went) there before.
4. Our class (go, goes) this week.
5. Ann and Jill (go, goes) together.
6. Tim (went, gone) last year.
7. We (go, goes) in the spring.
8. You (gone, went) with us.

Pronouns 31

- A **pronoun** is a word that takes the place of a noun.
- Pronouns that take the place of singular nouns are I, me, you, he, him, she, her, and it.
  EXAMPLE: **Dave** ate slowly. **He** ate slowly.
- Pronouns that take the place of plural nouns are we, us, you, they, and them.
  EXAMPLE: The popcorn is for **the boys.**
  The popcorn is for **them.**

- **Choose the correct pronoun in ( ) to take the place of the underlined noun. Then rewrite the sentences.**

1. Mrs. Cantu made popcorn for the class. (She, They)

   ____

2. Children love to eat popcorn. (She, They)

   ____

3. Hot air tosses popcorn around. (it, them)

   ____

4. Roger put salt on his popcorn. (He, They)

   ____

5. Don gave some popcorn to Colleen. (her, them)

   ____

6. Sue gave bowls to Bill and Bob. (it, them)

   ____

- **Write two sentences using pronouns.**

1. ______________________________
2. ______________________________

Subject and Object Pronouns 32

- Use these pronouns as **subjects:** I, you, he, she, it, we, and they. EXAMPLE: **I** like tall tales.
- Use these pronouns as **objects** that follow an action verb: me, you, him, her, it, us, and them.
  EXAMPLE: Paul Bunyan amazed **them.**

- **Write S if the underlined pronoun is used as a subject. Write O if it is used as an object.**

_____ 1. Davy Crockett beat him in a race.

_____ 2. We read about Mike Fink.

_____ 3. She told the tale in a whisper.

_____ 4. Pecos Bill kept them guessing.

_____ 5. It was a real adventure.

_____ 6. The blue ox surprised us.

- **Rewrite the sentences using a pronoun from the box in place of the underlined words.**

He	them	us	We

1. Jesse and I went to the rodeo.

____

2. The friendly cowgirl roped two calves.

____

3. The old man couldn't believe her strength.

____

4. The cowgirl gave Jesse and me a smile when she won.

____

Possessive Pronouns 33

- A **possessive pronoun** is a pronoun that shows who or what owns something. The pronouns my, our, your, his, her, its, and their are possessive pronouns.

  EXAMPLE: Ella rode **her** bike to school.

- **Underline the possessive pronoun in each sentence.**

1. Two monkeys did tricks for their trainers.
2. My family watched the monkeys.
3. Their names were Peg and Mike.
4. Peg tried to eat our lunch.
5. Then she put on her hat.
6. Mike clapped his hands.

- **Write the correct possessive pronoun in each blank.**

1. Bill lives in a house. ________________ house is white.
2. I live in an apartment. ________________ apartment has two bedrooms.
3. Sarah lives on a farm. ________________ farm is very big.
4. During the summer, Tom and Donna live on a houseboat.

   ________________ houseboat goes up and down the river.
5. My family has one car. ________________ car is old.
6. You have a new bike. ________________ bike is blue and white.
7. The tree is big. ________________ branches are long and thick.
8. Otis has a little brother. ________________ brother's name is Robert.

Using I or Me 34

- Use I in the subject of a sentence.
  EXAMPLE: **I** took Sara skating.
- Use me in the predicate of a sentence.
  EXAMPLE: Bev was waiting for **me.**
- Use I or me last when naming yourself and others.
  EXAMPLES: Juana and **I** like skating.
  Bev saw Otis and **me.**

- **Complete the sentences with the words in ( ). Be sure to put the words in the correct order.**

1. __________ and __________ wanted to go skating. (Liz, I)
2. Some of our friends were waiting for __________ and __________. (me, her)
3. Sal went with __________ and __________. (me, Liz)
4. __________ and __________ had a great time. (Liz, I)
5. __________ and __________ helped our friend Karen learn to skate. (I, Sal)
6. __________ and __________ held Karen's arms until she got to the rail. (I, Sal)
7. Karen smiled at __________ and __________. (me, Sal)
8. Then __________ and __________ gave Karen a little push to get her started. (I, Sal)
9. Karen thanked __________ and __________ for helping her learn to skate. (me, Sal)
10. __________ and __________ were happy about that! (I, Sal)

Adjectives 35

■ An **adjective** is a word that describes a noun or a pronoun. It tells which one, how many, or what kind.
EXAMPLE: The **two** clocks made a **loud** ring.

■ **Underline the adjectives.**

1. The bright sunlight peeked through the window.
2. The noisy alarm woke me up.
3. It was a great day for the carnival.
4. I threw on my old clothes.
5. Three friends met me at school.
6. Funny clowns walked in the yard.

■ **Complete the sentences with adjectives from the list.**

big	empty	little	top
brown	first	muddy	white
cold	gold	new	clean
deep	happy	red	old

1. Ron won a ________________ bear and a ________________ cat.
2. Ann won a ________________ tank with ________________ fish in it.
3. The ________________ girl chose a prize on the ________________ shelf.
4. A balloon had a ________________ bird and a ________________ dog on it.

Comparing with Adjectives 36

- Add -er to most adjectives to compare two persons, places, or things.
  EXAMPLE: The rabbit was **smaller** than the hat.
- Add -est to most adjectives to compare more than two persons, places, or things.
  EXAMPLE: That is the **smallest** rabbit I've seen.

- **Underline the correct form of the adjective in each sentence.**

1. The magician's show was (longer, longest) than the clown's.
2. The clown's shoes were the (funnier, funniest) of all the shoes.
3. The stage was the (bigger, biggest) one I've ever seen.
4. Our laughs were the (louder, loudest) in the crowd.
5. Our seats were the (closer, closest) to the stage.
6. The tightrope was (higher, highest) than a building.

- **Add -er or -est to the underlined adjective. Write the new words.**

1. The hand is quick than the eye. ____________________
2. That magician is the great in the world. ____________________
3. This is the proud moment of his life. ____________________
4. The white bird is light than the rabbit. ____________________
5. The rabbit is soft than the bird. ____________________
6. That trick is old than this country. ____________________

Using *A* or *An* 37

- Use a before words that begin with a consonant sound. EXAMPLES: a child, a fresh egg
- Use an before words that begin with a vowel sound. EXAMPLES: an adult, an old egg

- **Write a or an.**

1. _____ barn	**11.** _____ old barn
2. _____ apple	**12.** _____ red apple
3. _____ doctor	**13.** _____ good doctor
4. _____ test	**14.** _____ easy test
5. _____ adventure	**15.** _____ happy adventure
6. _____ balloon	**16.** _____ orange balloon
7. _____ animal	**17.** _____ clown's act
8. _____ bedroom	**18.** _____ upstairs room
9. _____ door	**19.** _____ open door
10. _____ house	**20.** _____ old house

- **Write a or an to complete this poem.**

The ostrich didn't see—

_____ cat,

_____ elephant,

_____ owl,

or a lion!

It saw another ostrich!

Adverbs 38

- An **adverb** is a word that describes a verb. It tells how, when, or where. Many adverbs end in -ly.

  EXAMPLES: The turtle crawled **slowly. How?**

  The turtle crawled **today. When?**

  The turtle crawled **there. Where?**

carefully
early everywhere
far happily here
later now quickly
quietly then out

- **The words above are adverbs. Write each word under a heading below to show if the word tells how, when, or where.**

HOW?	WHEN?	WHERE?
______	______	______
______	______	______
______	______	______
______	______	______

- **Underline each adverb. Write how, when, or where.**

1. Shawn eats breakfast early. ______
2. Andy walked quietly. ______
3. We will eat later. ______
4. The bird flew there. ______

Using *Good/Well* 39

- Use the adjective good to mean "better than average."
  EXAMPLE: We had a **good** time.
- Use the adverb well to mean "in a good way."
  EXAMPLE: No one slept very **well.**

- **Write good or well.**

1. We saw a ____________ movie at the sleepover.
2. Carmen danced very ____________.
3. Everyone had a ____________ time.
4. Lisa knows how to bake quite ____________.
5. She made a ____________ pizza for us.

- **Use good or well correctly in these paragraphs.**

Benny did not have a ____________ time when he was ill. But the doctor did his job ____________, so soon Benny was able to go outside. He went to a ____________ beach to surf.

His ____________ friend Marty went with him. Marty could surf very ____________. They ran into the water and waited for a ____________ wave. It was a ____________ day for surfing.

Benny and Marty get along ____________ and always have a ____________ time together.

Review

- **Underline the singular nouns. Circle the plural nouns.**

1. The garden will be full of flowers.
2. The children will mow the yard.
3. The roses are in the sun.
4. The birds love the birdbath.

- **Underline the common nouns. Circle the proper nouns.**

1. Greg scattered the seeds.
2. We'll have corn in September.

- **Underline the action verb. Circle the linking verb. Write present or past on the lines.**

1. The daisies grow quickly. ______________________
2. The roses were droopy. ______________________

- **Underline the correct verb.**

1. A bee (rests, rest) in a flower.
2. I (am, is, are) happy about the garden.
3. The rain (has, have) helped the plants grow.

- **Underline the correct pronoun.**

1. (She, Her) took a break.
2. This is (her, she) sandwich.
3. Mary and (I, me) climbed a tree.
4. We were in (we, our) yard.

- **Underline each adjective that compares.**

1. This leaf is the darkest on the twig.
2. Your dog is older than my dog.

- **Underline the adverbs.**

1. The carrots grew quickly.
2. The rain is falling lightly.
3. We'll have blossoms soon.
4. The sun shines brightly.

Using What You've Learned

- **The underlined words in the paragraph below are wrong. Rewrite the paragraph correctly.**

Monster Mack is looking at himself in the mirror. Her hair look like dry grass. It need to be cut. Our brown eyes flash and sparkles in the bright light. The smile on his face are like a half moon. It disappear when you see his nose. His nose is smallest than his ears. It are good that her ears are huge, though. Them get everyone's attention when he wiggle they.

- Write a funny paragraph describing another monster. Then go back and circle two singular or plural nouns, two common or proper nouns, an action verb, a helping verb, two pronouns, three adjectives, and two adverbs. If you don't have all of these, add them to your paragraph.

Capitalizing Days, Holidays, and Months **40**

- Use a **capital letter** to begin proper nouns, such as days of the week, months, or holidays.
  EXAMPLES: Monday, Friday, February, May, Thanksgiving, Labor Day
- Use a **small letter** to begin the name of each season.
  EXAMPLES: spring, summer, fall, winter

- **Rewrite the words. Use capital letters where they are needed.**

1. mother's day ________________
2. winter ________________
3. july ________________
4. saturday ________________
5. june ________________
6. halloween ________________
7. thursday ________________
8. april ________________

- **Rewrite the sentences. Use capital letters where they are needed.**

1. This fall I am having a halloween party.

____

____

2. The party is in october.

____

3. Last winter I had a party on valentine's day.

____

____

4. Is your birthday on friday this year?

____

Capitalizing Names of People and Places 41

- Use a capital letter to begin each word in proper nouns, such as names of people, family names, and place names.
  EXAMPLES: Gary Woodlawn, Grandma Cary, Kansas City, Vermont
- Use a small letter to begin a family name that comes after words like my, your, and their.
  EXAMPLES: their uncle, my grandma

- **Rewrite the words. Use capital letters where they are needed.**

1. uncle brian ____________________
2. new york ____________________
3. jamie smith ____________________
4. my grandfather ____________________
5. dallas ____________________
6. florida ____________________
7. aunt dee ____________________
8. charles ____________________
9. iowa ____________________
10. chicago ____________________

- **Rewrite the sentences. Use capital letters where they are needed.**

1. We put on a play about ramona quimby.

____

2. Did your uncle from san diego see it?

____

3. I think aunt lil liked it.

____

4. susan allen had the part of ramona.

____

Beginning Sentences

42

- Use a capital letter to begin the first word of a sentence. EXAMPLE: The pony licked her hand.

- **Write the sentences. Use a capital letter to begin each sentence.**

1. would you like to have a pony?

2. elena has a pretty red pony.

3. her pony's name is Rosie.

4. she rides her pony every day.

5. it is tiny, but fast.

6. the pony races through the fields.

7. elena brushes her pony.

8. then it takes a nap.

9. a pony is a fun pet.

Ending Sentences

43

- Use a **period** (**.**) at the end of a sentence that tells something.
  EXAMPLE: Ron has a new guppy**.**
- Use a **question mark** (**?**) at the end of a sentence that asks a question.
  EXAMPLE: Did he name it**?**
- Use an **exclamation point** (**!**) at the end of a sentence that shows strong feelings.
  EXAMPLE: What a good swimmer it is**!**

- **Use a period, question mark, or exclamation point at the end of each sentence.**

1. Guppies can live in a large bowl of water
2. Does the water need to be cleaned
3. Look at all the baby guppies
4. Can you count how many there are
5. What a pretty tail that guppy has

- **Write the sentences. End each one with a period, question mark, or exclamation point.**

1. Do you feed guppies dry food

____

2. I can't believe how well they swim

____

3. The biggest guppy is named Butch

____

4. What is the little one's name

____

5. I like him the best

____

Abbreviating Names of People and Places 44

- An **abbreviation** is the shortened form of a word.
- Use a capital letter to begin an abbreviation for a title of respect or an abbreviation for the name of a place. Use a period at the end of these abbreviations.
  EXAMPLES: Ms., Mrs., Mr., Dr., Yellow Brick Rd.
- An **initial** is the first letter of a name. Capitalize an initial and put a period after it.
  EXAMPLE: M. C. Livingston for Molly Coe Livingston

- **Write the names. Correct the initials and the abbreviations that are underlined. Use capital letters and periods where they are needed.**

1. Laura i Wilder ______________________
2. mrs Tolan ______________________
3. Cherry Tree rd ______________________
4. dr Doolittle ______________________
5. a a Milne ______________________
6. ms t Lowry ______________________
7. Quimby st ______________________
8. mrs Banks ______________________
9. e m Thomas ______________________

- **Circle the mistakes in the sentence below. Write each correction on a line.**

miss Binney is in a book by b Cleary.

1. ______________ 2. ______________

Abbreviating Names of Days and Months 45

- Use capital letters to begin abbreviations for days of the week. Use periods at the end of the abbreviations.
  EXAMPLES: Sun., Mon., Wed., Thurs., Sat.
- Use capital letters to begin abbreviations for months of the year. Use periods at the end of the abbreviations.
  EXAMPLES: Jan., Feb., Apr., Aug., Nov., Dec.

- **Write the abbreviations for the days and the months. Use capital letters and periods where they are needed.**

1. Thursday ____________
2. August ____________
3. Sunday ____________
4. March ____________
5. Tuesday ____________
6. February ____________
7. Monday ____________
8. September ____________
9. October ____________
10. Saturday ____________
11. December ____________
12. Wednesday ____________
13. November ____________
14. Friday ____________
15. January ____________
16. April ____________

- **Circle the mistakes in the sentences below. Write each correction on a line.**

1. Lee asked me to a party on sat, sept 4th.

   ____________ ____________

2. I'm having a party on fri, oct 31st.

   ____________ ____________

Using Commas in Sentences 46

- Use a **comma** (,) after the words yes and no if they begin a sentence. EXAMPLES: Yes, I saw the clowns at the parade. No, I didn't see them dance.
- Use a comma to separate three or more items listed together in a sentence. EXAMPLE: The float was red, white, and blue.

- **Write the sentences. Use commas where they are needed.**

1. Yes the band was in the parade.

2. Patty Carlos and Jo rode on a float.

3. We saw the bands clowns and floats.

4. Horses fire engines and flags came next.

5. No I didn't stay until the end.

6. Yes I wanted to stay.

7. We bought juice nuts and fruit to eat.

8. Yes I waved to the woman on the horse.

9. No she didn't see me.

Writing Letters Correctly 47

- Use a comma between numbers for the day and year in the **heading** of a letter. EXAMPLE: June 26, 1989
- Use a comma between the city and state in an **address.** EXAMPLE: Carbondale, Illinois 62901
- Use a capital letter to begin the first word and all names in the **greeting** of a letter. Use a comma at the end of the greeting. EXAMPLE: Dear Mom,
- Use a capital letter to begin only the first word in the **closing** of a letter. Use a comma at the end of the closing. EXAMPLE: Very truly yours,

- **Circle the words that should be capitalized in the letter. Add commas where needed.**

34 High Rise Street
New York New York 10011
April 3 1990

dear gina

your friend

Danielle

- **Rewrite these parts of a letter. Use capital letters and commas where they are needed.**

1. May 7 1989 ______________________________

2. Miami Florida 33137 ______________________________

3. dear alicia ______________

4. with love ______________

Using Apostrophes to Show Ownership 48

- Add an **apostrophe** (') and -s ('s) to nouns like girl to show that one person owns something.
  EXAMPLE: the **girl's** present
- Add an apostrophe after nouns like girls to show that more than one person owns something.
  EXAMPLE: the **girls'** presents
- Add an apostrophe and -s ('s) to plural nouns like children to show that more than one person owns something. EXAMPLE: the **children's** presents

- **Rewrite each phrase to show ownership. Add an apostrophe or an apostrophe and -s to the underlined words.**

1. the pilot hat

   ____

2. the woman car

   ____

3. five dogs bones

   ____

4. a kittens toys

   ____

5. a clown hat

   ____

6. many mens hats

   ____

7. the women cars

   ____

8. a snowman nose

   ____

9. ten kites strings

   ____

10. the birds nests

    ____

- **Write a sentence telling about something that belongs to a friend or friends. Use an apostrophe or an apostrophe and -s to show who owns it.**

____

____

Using Apostrophes in Contractions 49

- A **contraction** is a word made by joining two words.
- Use an apostrophe to show that letters are left out.

  EXAMPLES: **it's** = it is **hasn't** = has not

- **Write contractions for the pairs of words. Leave out the letters that are underlined.**

1. she + is ____________
2. we + are ____________
3. you + will ____________
4. I + have ____________
5. he + would ____________
6. she + has ____________

- **Write contractions for the pairs of words.**

1. has + not ____________
2. is + not ____________
3. were + not ____________
4. I + will ____________
5. that + is ____________
6. would + not ____________
7. they + will ____________
8. there + is ____________

- **Rewrite the sentences. Use contractions for the words that are underlined.**

1. Jay has not seen that movie.

   ____

2. It is about a strange land.

   ____

3. One year winter does not come.

   ____

4. The people do not mind.

   ____

Using Quotation Marks **50**

- Use **quotation marks** (“ ”) before and after the words a speaker says. EXAMPLE: Mother said, “I’m going to leave for about an hour.”
- Use a comma between the words the speaker says and the rest of the sentence. Put the comma before the quotation marks. Capitalize the first word the speaker says. EXAMPLES: “We’re leaving now,” said Mother. **or** Mother said, “We’re leaving now.”

- **Read the cartoon. Think about who is talking and what they are saying.**

- **Answer the questions about the cartoon. Use quotation marks and commas where needed.**

1. What did Carl say first?

   “Yes, I will,” said Carl. **or** Carl said, “Yes, I will.”

2. What did Jane say first?

3. What did Jane say about the butter?

4. What was the last thing Carl said?

Review

- **Correct the sentences. Circle letters that should be capitalized. Put periods, question marks, and commas where they are needed.**

1. mr and mrs kamp lived in a house on may street
2. one saturday the family cleaned the attic
3. ella found an old letter from dr r m wilson
4. we found a picture of roses daisies and tulips
5. did dad take that photo on valentine's day
6. yes mom will clean out the attic next spring

- **Rewrite the abbreviations. Use capital letters and periods where needed.**

1. tues ____________________
2. fri ____________________
3. mrs ____________________
4. elm st ____________________
5. jan ____________________
6. m c lee ____________________

- **Add commas to these parts of a letter. Circle the small letters that should be capital letters.**

1. birmingham alabama 35205
2. august 18 1989
3. dear kim
4. yours truly

- **Add apostrophes, quotation marks, and commas to these sentences where they are needed.**

1. This is Ellas game said Louisa.
2. Tom said Its the childrens favorite.
3. It isnt hard to play.

Using What You've Learned

- **Correct the story. As you read it, circle letters that should be capitals. Put periods, question marks, exclamation points, commas, apostrophes, and quotation marks where they are needed. Rewrite the title and the story on the lines.**

A Hidden Surprise

jills cat is named sam____ what a big smart beautiful cat he is____ one summer day jill couldnt find him____ do you know where he was____ he was under the porch with three new kittens____ jill said your name is samantha now____

- Write a letter to Jill. Tell her what you think about her surprise. Use your address and today's date in the heading. Write a greeting and a closing. Be sure to use an abbreviation and a contraction in your letter. Use capital letters, periods, question marks, exclamation points, commas, and apostrophes. Check your letter for any mistakes.

Writing Sentences 51

- A **sentence** must tell a complete thought.
- Remember to begin a sentence with a capital letter and end it with a period, a question mark, or an exclamation point.

  EXAMPLE: **Thought:** making our puppets
  Sentence: We are making puppets.

- **Write each of these thoughts about making a puppet as a sentence.**

1. finding some yarn for our puppet's hair

____

2. cutting yarn for the puppet's hair

____

3. gluing the yarn to our puppet's head

____

4. making a face on the puppet's head

____

5. making a costume for our puppet

____

6. sewing buttons on the costume

____

7. dressing the puppet

____

8. putting shoes on the puppet

____

9. using the puppet in a puppet show

____

Writing Paragraphs 52

- A **paragraph** is a group of sentences about one main idea. **Indent** the first line. To indent a paragraph, leave a space before the first word.
- A paragraph should have sentences about the same subject.

  EXAMPLE:

  Last night my brother and I put on a puppet show. We invited our parents and our little sister, Becky. Dad made popcorn, and everyone laughed.

- **Read the paragraph. Then write another paragraph. Tell what else you think happened in this puppet show. Be sure to indent.**

My brother's puppet was named Morris. My puppet was Garfield. Morris was a fussy cat, and Garfield was his funny friend. Morris wouldn't eat much. Garfield loved to eat. Garfield asked my family to share their popcorn with him. Everyone agreed to share.

Writing Topic Sentences 53

- A **topic sentence** tells the main idea, or topic, of a paragraph.
- All sentences in a paragraph should be about that topic.

  EXAMPLE: Liquid soap bottles make wonderful hand puppets. Just turn the bottle upside down, and paint a face on the bottom part. If you wish, glue a piece of cloth around the middle of the bottle. Stick your finger in the top of the bottle. There's your puppet!

- **Underline the topic sentence in each paragraph.**

Many people are needed to put on a puppet show. Someone must make the puppets and the set. Others must move the puppets and act in the show. Someone is needed to seat people and dim the lights.

Shadow puppets are different from other kinds of puppets. You look at the shadow of the puppet instead of the puppet. The puppets are held and moved in front of a light so their shadows look alive.

The person holding the puppet makes the puppet move. Some puppets move by strings that can be pulled. Others fit over a hand and move when the hand moves. Some puppets seem to talk when they are held the right way.

Writing Details 54

- **Details** after the topic sentence in a paragraph should tell more about the main idea.

  EXAMPLE: Liquid soap bottles make wonderful hand puppets. Just turn the bottle upside down, and paint a face on the bottom part. If you wish, glue a piece of cloth around the middle of the bottle. Stick your finger in the top of the bottle. There's your puppet!

- **Circle the topic sentence. Underline the four sentences that give details about the main idea. Write the circled and underlined sentences in a new paragraph.**

Our puppet show was a great success. Parents, friends, and neighbors came to see it. I am going to learn how to swim this summer. Altogether, we sold twenty tickets and made $10.00. Rita already knows how to swim. Everyone liked the show and clapped for about two minutes after it was over. My uncle's name is Tony. He knows how to swim well. A good time was had by all!

Arranging Details in Order 55

- The details in a paragraph can be arranged in different ways. One way to arrange details is to put them in the **order** in which they happen.
- Words such as first, next, then, and finally help to show order.

  EXAMPLE: To make a ball-and-pencil puppet, **first** punch a sharp pencil into a soft ball. **Next,** wrap a piece of cloth just under the ball. **Then** tie a ribbon around the top part of the cloth. **Finally,** glue yarn hair on the ball and draw a face with markers.

- **Write numbers to show the right order in the paragraphs.**

_____ Next, give the people a program that lists the puppet characters. _____ Finally, call out, "Let the show begin!" _____ First, collect the tickets on the night of the big show. _____ Then when everyone is seated, dim the lights. _____ Help people find their seats in the audience.

_____ Next, the piano music started. _____ Then two puppets, a clown, and a donkey sang to the music. _____ Finally, the curtain came down. _____ First, the curtain went up. _____ Everyone laughed and clapped when the donkey sang "Hee-Haw."

Writing with Purpose 56

- **Purpose** in writing is the reason why something is written.
- One purpose is to tell about a thought or feeling.
  EXAMPLE: I thought I'd never stop laughing.
- Another purpose is to describe something.
  EXAMPLE: The bright red color of the bird shone through the waving branches of the trees.
- Another purpose is to give information.
  EXAMPLE: The science fair is today.
- Another purpose is to tell about something that is make-believe.
  EXAMPLE: The snowflakes talked to one another as they fell to the ground.

- **Write a sentence that tells how you feel about going to puppet shows.**

____

- **Write a sentence that describes a puppet.**

____

____

- **Write a sentence that gives some information about a puppet show.**

____

____

- **Write the first sentence of a make-believe story that could be used for a puppet show.**

____

____

Choosing a Topic 57

Here are some steps to follow in choosing a **topic.**

- Write a list of persons, things, or animals that interest you. Then circle the topic that especially interests you.

  EXAMPLES: clowns, (putting on a puppet show), tigers
- Divide the topic into smaller parts. Choose the one that you would like to write about.

  EXAMPLES: making a princess puppet, sending out invitations, practicing for the show

- **You are going to write a paragraph. Your purpose is to give someone information about how to make something. You need to choose a topic. Write a list of different things you can make.**

1. ______
2. ______
3. ______
4. ______
5. ______
6. ______

- **Circle the topic that especially interests you.**

- **Divide the topic you circled into smaller parts. Underline the one you would like to write about.**

1. ______
2. ______
3. ______
4. ______
5. ______
6. ______

How-to Paragraph 58

- The purpose of some paragraphs is to give instructions.
- A **how-to paragraph** tells how to do something.

EXAMPLE:

How to Make a Soap-Bottle King Puppet

It is not hard to make a soap-bottle king puppet. To begin, search through your house for materials to make your puppet. You will need to find a dishwashing soap bottle, scrap cloth, paper, and markers. First, make the puppet head by turning the bottle upside down. Draw a face and hair on the bottle with markers. Next, glue a paper crown above the face. Then glue a piece of scrap cloth around the middle of the bottle. Put your finger in the opening of the bottle, and say "Hello" to the king.

- **Write the topic sentence for the paragraph in the box.**

____

- **Write four sentences that give details about the topic.**

____

____

____

____

____

____

____

Writing a How-to Paragraph 59

- Look at the topic you chose on page 69. Write a how-to paragraph about your topic. Use the model on page 70 to help you. Be sure to include a good topic sentence and the steps you would follow.

Writing an Invitation 60

- An **invitation** is a kind of letter. An invitation tells the following things: **who** will give the event, **what** kind of event it will be, **when** it will begin and end, and **where** it will take place.
- An invitation includes the address or telephone number of the sender.

EXAMPLE:

569 North Street
Akron, Ohio 44305
August 6, 19___

Dear Jesse,

Please come to a puppet show on Saturday, August 20. It will be at May Baldwin's house, 22 Oak Avenue, from 3:00 to 4:00. See you then!

Your neighbor,
Craig

Call 555-6340

- **Write an invitation to a party you would like to have.**

Writing a Telephone Message 61

- A **telephone message** tells:
  1. The **day** and **time** the message was received.
  2. The **name** of the person getting the message.
  3. The **name** of the person who called.
  4. The **phone number** of the person who called.
  5. The important **information** from the call.
  6. The **name** of the person who took the message.

  EXAMPLE:

  4/18/89
  10:15 a.m.

  Jay—

  Beth Bishop called and wants you to call her back at 555-3958. She needs to ask you how to make soap-bottle puppets for her play.

  Fran

- **Read this part of a telephone call. Then write the message Hannah might leave for Terry. Write today's date and time.**

HANNAH: "Terry isn't home. I'll take a message for her."

NAN: "Please tell her to call me back at 555-2749.
I want her to get some cloth for the puppets
we're making. Thanks. Good-bye."

(Date) ______________________

(Time) ______________________

(To) ______________________

(Message) ____

____

(From) ______________________

Review

- **Write each thought as a sentence.**

1. putting the puppet on my hand

____

2. making the puppet nod its head

____

3. moving the puppet's mouth

____

- **Circle the topic sentence in the paragraph below. Then underline only the sentences that give details about the main idea.**

A break between acts in a play is needed. It allows time for the crowd to get up and stretch. Sarah is a very good math student. It lets the people in the show get ready for the rest of the play. And it gives time to prepare for the next act.

- **Write numbers to show the correct order of the details for each set of directions below.**

_____ Then let the popcorn pop. _____ First, pour popcorn into a pan. _____ Finally, serve it to the crowd. _____ Next, put a lid on top of the pan.

_____ Then mix the juice and water together. _____ Finally, pour the juice into glasses. _____ First, spoon frozen juice into a pitcher. _____ Next, add cold water.

Using What You've Learned

- **Read this story.**

One day Sam was looking for something fun to do. Sam decided he would like to ask his friend Ho to come over to play. Sam's mother said that he should call Ho after lunch. Sam was so excited, thinking about all the fun they'd have together. Since it was such a nice day, they would be able to play outside. Sam decided to ask Ho to bring his bike so that they could ride together.

- **Pretend that Ho is not home when Sam calls. Write a telephone message for Ho. Write the important information from the call. Use the correct names, today's date, the time, and your phone number.**

- **Write an invitation to a show that your class might put on.**

- **Write a how-to paragraph telling how to get to your school. Write a topic sentence and supporting details. Use words such as first, next, and then to put the details in order.**

Following Directions 62

- **Directions** must be followed step-by-step.
- Sometimes maps help you to follow directions. They might show which way is north, south, east, and west by the letters N, S, E, and W.

EXAMPLE:

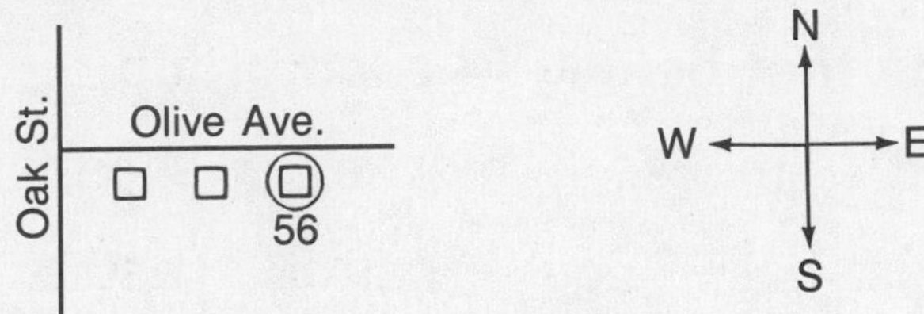

Directions to May's House

1) Go north on Oak Street.
2) Turn east on Olive Avenue.
3) Walk 3 houses down to 56 Olive Avenue.

- **Look at the map, and read the directions to Harry's house. Then answer the questions.**

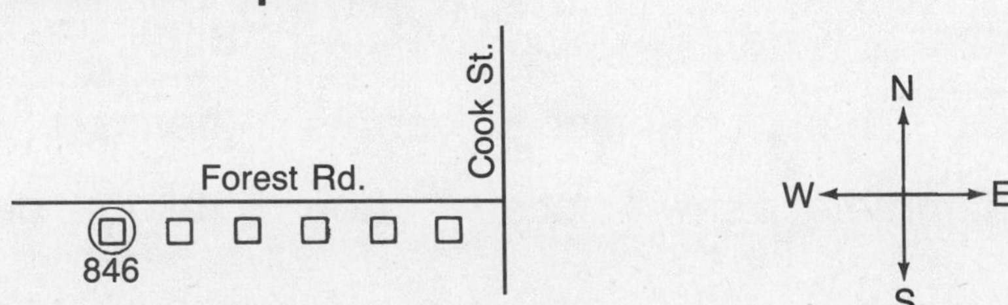

1) Go south on Cook Street.
2) Turn west on Forest Road.
3) Walk down 6 houses to 846 Forest Road.

1. What direction should you go first? ____________________

2. What street should you walk on first? ____________________

3. What direction should you go next? ____________________

4. What street would you be on? ____________________

5. How many houses down Forest Road is Harry's house? ____________________

Grouping 63

- Things that are alike in some way can be **grouped** together. The name of the group tells how the things in the group are alike.
  EXAMPLE: Dogs, cats, and horses are all animals.

- **Underline the words that belong in each group.**

1. **animals** sand mouse monkey sheep flower bird
2. **foods** bread hat egg carrot apple fish
3. **colors** blue red grass purple orange cow
4. **fruits** apple cake orange milk banana grape
5. **clothes** pants foot shirt jacket pale hat
6. **round things** ball desk circle rake penny orange
7. **flying things** bike bird jet snake rocket turtle
8. **boys' names** Peter Ann Mike Jill Josh Tom
9. **girls' names** Karen David Pam Bill Elaine Melanie
10. **vegetables** peas apples carrots beans corn tuna
11. **tools** hammer saw chair hoe rake desk

- **Write the words below under the correct heading.**

monkey	school	potato
carrot	elephant	store
house	corn	lion

Zoo Animals	Vegetables	Buildings
______	______	______
______	______	______
______	______	______

Parts of a Book 64

- The **table of contents** is in the front of a book. It lists titles and page numbers of parts of the book.

  EXAMPLE:

  Synonyms 1

  Antonyms 2

- The **index** is in the back of a book. It lists the subjects of the book in alphabetical order and gives page numbers.

  EXAMPLE:

  Abbreviations, 53, 54, 60, 61

  Action verbs, 28, 40, 48

- **Use the table of contents in this book to answer the questions.**

1. How many units are in this book? ____________________
2. What is the title of Unit 5? ____________________
3. On what page is “Using Commas in Sentences” in Unit 4? __________
4. What is the title of page 13? ____________________
5. On what page is “Writing Sentences” in Unit 5? ____________
6. What is the title of page 46? ____________________

- **Use the index of this book to answer the questions.**

1. What pages tell about suffixes? ____________________
2. What pages tell about antonyms? ____________________
3. What pages tell about quotation marks? ________________
4. Are the words business letters listed in the index? __________

Alphabetical Order 65

- **Alphabetical order** is the order of the letters in the alphabet. To put words in alphabetical order, look at the first letter of each word. Use the first letter of each word to put the words in the order of the alphabet.
  EXAMPLES: **b**ag, **p**ack, **c**ottage = **b**ag, **c**ottage, **p**ack
- Look at the second letter if the words begin with the same letter.
  EXAMPLES: f**i**sh, f**r**y, f**e**ast = f**e**ast, f**i**sh, f**r**y

- **Write each set of words in alphabetical order.**

oar canoe paddle	giant good glass
1. ______	**1.** ______
2. ______	**2.** ______
3. ______	**3.** ______

town week ranch	bounce ball beach
1. ______	**1.** ______
2. ______	**2.** ______
3. ______	**3.** ______

east soap dream	pole price pump
1. ______	**1.** ______
2. ______	**2.** ______
3. ______	**3.** ______

Guide Words

66

- **Guide words** are at the top of each dictionary page. They show the first and last words on the page. Every word listed on the page comes between the guide words.

  EXAMPLE: **oak / real**

oak	~~~~~
ocean	ready
~~	real

- **Write the pair of guide words that each word comes between.**

add / chase **quack / weep**

1. beehive add / chase
2. reason ______
3. wall ______
4. attach ______
5. usual ______
6. cabin ______
7. quiet ______
8. spark ______

- **Write the word that would be on the same page with each set of guide words.**

iron	across	ill	dine	dad	job
arrow	weight	ship	wonder	herd	post

1. idea / in ______
2. apple / ax ______
3. different / dry ______
4. jar / just ______
5. insect / island ______
6. wagon / winter ______
7. cut / desk ______
8. serve / space ______
9. able / ago ______
10. wheat / wrong ______
11. hair / hose ______
12. pine / price ______

Using Dictionary Definitions 67

- Words that are listed on a dictionary page are called **entry words.** They are listed in alphabetical order.
- A dictionary gives the **definition,** or meaning, for each entry word.
- Some words have more than one meaning. Then each meaning is numbered.

  EXAMPLE:

  easy **1.** not hard to do. **2.** free from trouble.

calf **1.** a young cow or bull. **2.** the young of other animals.

call **1.** to say in a loud voice. **2.** to give a name to. **3.** to make a telephone call.

carol a song.

carpet **1.** a floor covering made of heavy cloth. **2.** to cover an area completely.

- **Read the definitions of each entry word. Then answer the questions.**

1. Which word has one meaning? ____________________

2. Which word has three meanings? ____________________

3. Which words have two meanings? ____________________

4. Which word means "a song"? ____________________

5. Write a sentence with one meaning of carpet. ____________________

____

6. Write a sentence with one meaning of call. ____________________

____

7. Write a sentence with the first meaning of calf. ____________________

____

part 1. an amount less than the whole. **2.** the line made when hair is combed. **3.** an actor's role.
pass 1. to go by. **2.** to do the opposite of fail.
peace 1. freedom from war. **2.** quiet.
pen 1. something to write with. **2.** a place to keep animals.
place 1. space taken up by a person or thing. **2.** a city, town, country, or other area. **3.** to put.
plant 1. a living thing that is not an animal. **2.** to put something in the ground to grow.
point 1. a sharp end. **2.** a method of scoring in a game. **3.** the main idea or important part.

■ **The entry words in the box have more than one meaning. Write the number of the correct meaning next to each sentence.**

1. My old red pen ran out of ink. ____
2. Naomi couldn't find a place for her table. ____
3. They will plant daisies in the spring. ____
4. Arnold sat in the chair to get some peace. ____
5. Did most of the class pass the test? ____
6. Don't place the candles too near the heat. ____
7. What kind of plant are you growing? ____
8. The little pigs were in a pen. ____
9. Do you have to travel far to get to the place? ____
10. Did the car pass the truck? ____
11. Do the soldiers want peace or war? ____
12. Kirk scored ten points in basketball. ____
13. He only played for part of the game. ____
14. The teacher asks us to keep a point on our pencils. ____
15. Everyone had a part in our class play. ____
16. There was no part in her hair. ____

Review

- **Circle the words that belong in each group.**

1. **babies** puppy chick cat kitten lamb dog
2. **seasons** fall day spring summer rain winter
3. **fruit** beans apples oranges peas pears seeds

- **Name the group for each set of words.**

1. pants dress shirt skirt coat

____

2. lunch supper breakfast dinner

____

- **Write each list of words in alphabetical order.**

1. seen ________	2. blue ________	3. press ________
lake ________	bee ________	plow ________
cage ________	bat ________	puff ________

- **Read the dictionary entries for stalk and stand. Write the meaning that goes with each sentence below.**

stalk **1.** the stem of a plant. **2.** to hunt.
stand **1.** to be on one's feet. **2.** to put up with.

1. I watched the cat stalk the wind-up toy.

____

2. Let's stand up and stretch.

____

3. We put the stalk in water to keep the plant alive.

____

4. I can't stand the smell of onions.

____

Using What You've Learned

- **Imagine you are going shopping in a grocery store. To make your shopping trip quicker and easier, put the food items on the shopping list below into the groups in which they belong. Then answer the questions.**

Shopping List: canned soup, potatoes, bananas, frozen orange juice, lettuce, chicken, broccoli, carrots, hamburger, apples, bacon, canned tomatoes

Fruits	Canned	Vegetables
____________	____________	____________
____________	____________	____________
____________	____________	____________
____________	____________	____________

Frozen	Meat
____________	____________
____________	____________
____________	____________
____________	____________

1. What is the item in the frozen group? ____________
2. What groups have only two items? ____________
3. Which group has the most items? ____________
4. What items are in the meat group? ____________

   ____
5. Where did you list broccoli? ____________

- **Follow the directions to Della's house. Circle her house on the map.**

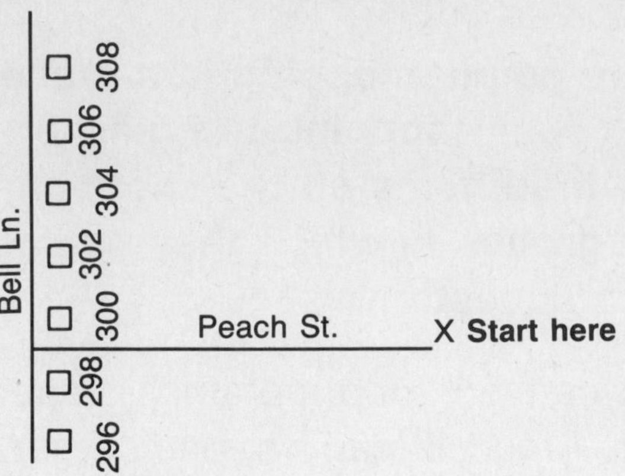

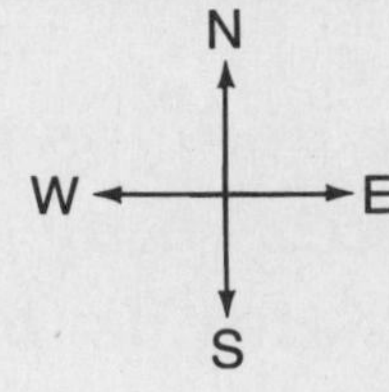

1. Go west on Peach Street.
2. Turn north on Bell Lane.
3. Go down 5 houses to 308 Bell Lane.

- **Write directions to 296 Bell Lane.**

____

____

____

- **Draw a map showing the street where you live. Draw a line to show what street crosses yours. Then write the directions to where you live.**

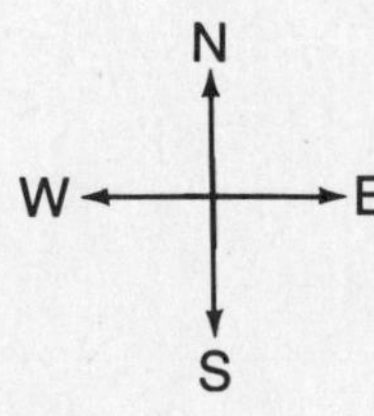

____

____

____

FINAL REVIEW

UNIT 1

Synonyms and Antonyms ▪ Write S if the underlined words are synonyms. Write A if they are antonyms.

_____ 1. The driver couldn't see through the thick fog and mist.

_____ 2. The gas tank went from full to empty in minutes.

_____ 3. We couldn't see to our right or to our left.

_____ 4. We had to stop on the side and wait for help because our car just wouldn't go anymore.

Homonyms ▪ Circle the correct homonym to complete each sentence.

1. We decided to stay (they're, their, there) and wait for help.
2. We hoped someone would bring (they're, their, there) car.
3. Soon we saw (two, too, to) headlights.
4. We could (hear, here) a siren coming closer.

Prefixes ▪ Underline the prefix. Write the meaning of the word.

1. unable ____________________
2. relive ____________________
3. repay ____________________
4. untrue ____________________

Compound Words and Contractions ▪ Make a compound word or a contraction from each pair of words. Circle the contractions.

1. some + one = ____________________
2. he + is = ____________________
3. I + will = ____________________
4. day + light = ____________________
5. is + not = ____________________
6. snow + storm = ____________________

FINAL REVIEW UNIT 2

Types of Sentences ▪ Write S for statement, Q for question, C for command, or E for exclamation for each sentence. Write X if the group of words is not a sentence.

_____ **1.** Rob played basketball.

_____ **2.** How many points did Lee make?

_____ **3.** What a good player she is!

_____ **4.** Pass the ball to Lupe.

_____ **5.** Scored ten points.

Subjects and Predicates ▪ Underline each subject. Circle each predicate.

1. The old net was torn.

2. Jay bounced the ball quickly.

3. Val picked up the pass.

4. Todd blocked the shot.

5. Carl jumped up for the ball.

6. The winners gave a cheer.

Combining Subjects and Predicates ▪ Combine the sentences. Write the new sentences.

1. Don signaled to Ed. Don passed the ball.

____

2. Vin wanted to play. Tammy wanted to play.

____

3. They won today. They lost last week.

____

4. Basketball is played inside. Football is played outside.

____

____

FINAL REVIEW

UNIT 3

Singular and Plural Nouns ▪ Write S before each singular noun. Then write its plural form. Write P before each plural noun. Then write its singular form.

_____ **1.** inches _____________________ _____ **4.** boxes _____________________

_____ **2.** toe _____________________ _____ **5.** cart _____________________

_____ **3.** bus _____________________ _____ **6.** tigers _____________________

Proper and Common Nouns ▪ Write P before each proper noun. Then write a common noun for it. Write C before each common noun. Then write a proper noun for it.

_____ **1.** friend _____________________ _____ **3.** school _____________________

_____ **2.** Texas _____________________ _____ **4.** Lake Erie _____________________

Verbs ▪ Underline each action verb. Circle each linking verb. Write present or past.

1. Katie lives in Chicago. _____________________

2. I visited her in June. _____________________

3. Diane was in Chicago last year. _____________________

Using the Correct Word ▪ Draw a line under the correct word.

1. Rory (runs, run) to catch the train.

2. He needed to (buy, buys) a ticket to Cleveland.

3. Rory (saw, seen) the train leaving suddenly.

4. (He, It) waved to get the train to stop.

5. The crowd (have, had) begun to leave.

6. So Rory (was, were) left alone at the station.

FINAL REVIEW

UNIT 4

Capitalizing Proper Nouns ▪ Rewrite the words. Use capital letters where needed.

1. december ______________________
2. winter ______________________
3. monday ______________________
4. my sister ______________________
5. mom ______________________
6. flag day ______________________
7. california ______________________
8. denver ______________________

Capitalization ▪ Circle the letters that should be capitalized.

1. the museum is near jones street.
2. it is called the charles c. adler museum.
3. mrs. kelly is taking our class there.
4. they are closed on mondays.
5. dinosaur bones are at the museum.
6. we're going on the first tuesday in march.

Punctuation ▪ Put periods, commas, question marks, quotation marks, and apostrophes where needed.

1. We saw dinosaur bones snakes and birds at the museum
2. We watched a film on dinosaur babies
3. Kai said Id like to come back to the museum soon
4. And I really liked it said Gail
5. I liked the filmstrip cave and footprints the best said Kai
6. Lets go again soon said the class
7. Lets plan a trip for next month said Mrs Kelly

Writing Sentences ▪ Write each thought as a sentence.

1. watching television after dinner

____

2. laughing at the funny lines

____

3. eating popcorn as I watch

____

Topic Sentence ▪ Circle the topic sentence in each paragraph. Underline each sentence that gives details about the main idea.

Yesterday Mrs. Ozu's class put on a television show. Everybody played a part. Some children acted. It was a warm day. Others held make-believe cameras. Still others just had a good time watching the show.

Most people get scared when they have to act in front of people. You will feel better if you get used to being on a stage. It is good practice to be in class plays and shows. Shirley Temple was a famous young actress. The more you're on a stage, the less scared you feel.

Arranging Details in Order ▪ Write numbers to show the right order of the details.

_____ Next, choose a channel. _____ First, turn on the television. _____ Then sit back and watch the show.

FINAL REVIEW UNIT 6

Grouping ▪ Underline the words that belong in each group.

1. **months** July May Friday March Tuesday April
2. **weather** wind rain clouds sun snow airplane

Write the words below under the correct heading.

toast	spaghetti	pancakes
fish	popcorn	raisins

Breakfast	Dinner	Snacks
________	________	________
________	________	________

Alphabetical Order ▪ Write each list of words in alphabetical order.

1. rake ________ 2. teeth ________
   scare ________ cause ________
   sat ________ cheer ________

Guide Words ▪ Study the dictionary page at the right. Write the guide words for the page.

leather ... lie

________ / ________

Words with More Than One Meaning ▪ Read the dictionary entry for batter. Write the number of the meaning that goes with each sentence.

1. Paco mixed the batter for two minutes. ____
2. The second batter hit a home run. ____

batter 1. a mixture of flour, milk, and eggs used in cooking. **2.** a player whose turn it is to bat.